ECDL® 5.0

European Computer Driving Licence

Module 7a - Web Browsing
using Internet Explorer 6

This training, which has been approved by ECDL Foundation, includes exercise items intended to assist Candidates in their training for an ECDL Certification Programme. These exercises are not ECDL Foundation certification tests. For information about authorised Test Centres in different national territories, please refer to the ECDL Foundation website at www.ecdl.org

Release ECDL254v1

Published by:

CiA Training Ltd
Business & Innovation Centre
Sunderland Enterprise Park
Sunderland SR5 2TH
United Kingdom

Tel: +44 (0) 191 549 5002
Fax: +44 (0) 191 549 9005

E-mail: info@ciatraining.co.uk
Web: www.ciatraining.co.uk

ISBN-13: 978 1 86005 680 2

The following information applies only to candidates in Ireland.

Acknowledgements:

The European Computer Driving Licence is operated in Ireland by ICS Skills, the training and certification body of the Irish Computer Society.
Candidates using this courseware should register online with ICS Skills through an approved ECDL Test Centre. Without a valid registration, and the allocation of a unique ICS Skills ID number or SkillsCard, no ECDL tests can be taken and no certificate, or any other form of recognition, can be given to a candidate.

Other ECDL Foundation Certification programmes offered by ICS Skills include Equalskills, ECDL Advanced, ECDL WebStarter, ECDL ImageMaker, EUCIP and Certified Training Professional.

Contact: ICS Skills
Crescent Hall
Mount Street Crescent
Dublin 2
Ireland

Website: www.ics.ie/skills

Email: *skills@ics.ie*

First published 2008

CiA Training Ltd is an entity independent of ECDL Foundation and is not associated with ECDL Foundation in any manner. This courseware may be used to assist candidates to prepare for the ECDL Foundation Certification Programme as titled on the courseware. Neither ECDL Foundation nor **CiA Training Ltd** warrants that the use of this courseware publication will ensure passing of the tests for that ECDL Foundation Certification Programme. This courseware publication has been independently reviewed and approved by ECDL Foundation as covering the learning objectives for the ECDL Foundation Certification Programme.

Confirmation of this approval can be obtained by reviewing the Partners Page in the About Us Section of the website www.ecdl.org

The material contained in this courseware publication has not been reviewed for technical accuracy and does not guarantee that candidates will pass the test for the ECDL Foundation Certification Programme. Any and all assessment items and/or performance-based exercises contained in this courseware relate solely to this publication and do not constitute or imply certification by ECDL Foundation in respect of the ECDL Foundation Certification Programme or any other ECDL Foundation test. Irrespective of how the material contained in this courseware is deployed, for example in a learning management system (LMS) or a customised interface, nothing should suggest to the candidate that this material constitutes certification or can lead to certification through any other process than official ECDL Foundation certification testing.

For details on sitting a test for an ECDL Foundation certification programme, please contact your country's designated National Licensee or visit the ECDL Foundation's website at www.ecdl.org.

Candidates using this courseware must be registered with the National Operator before undertaking a test for an ECDL Foundation Certification Programme. Without a valid registration, the test(s) cannot be undertaken and no certificate, nor any other form of recognition, can be given to a candidate. Registration should be undertaken with your country's designated National Licensee at an Approved Test Centre.

Downloading the Data Files

The data associated with these exercises must be downloaded from our website. Go to: ***www.ciatraining.co.uk/data***. Follow the on screen instructions to download the appropriate data files.

By default, the data files will be downloaded to **My Documents \ CIA DATA FILES \ ECDL**.

If you prefer, the data can be supplied on CD at an additional cost. Contact the Sales team at ***info@ciatraining.co.uk***.

Aims

To demonstrate the ability to use web browser on a personal computer. To understand and accomplish basic operations associated with searching and navigating web sites to access information.

Objectives

After completing the guide the user will be able to:

- Understand what the Internet is and common terms associated with it; be aware of some security considerations when using the Internet. Accomplish everyday web browsing tasks including changing browser settings
- Complete and submit web-based forms and search for information; save web pages and download files from the web. Copy web content into a document

Assessment of Knowledge

At the end of this guide is a section called the **Record of Achievement Matrix**. Before the guide is started it is recommended that the user complete the matrix to measure the level of current knowledge.

Tick boxes are provided for each feature. **1** is for no knowledge, **2** some knowledge and **3** is for competent.

After working through a section, complete the **Record of Achievement** matrix for that section and only when competent in all areas move on to the next section.

Contents

Section 1 Getting Started

By the end of this Section you should be able to:

Understand the Internet

Be Aware of Security Issues

Use Internet Explorer

Connect and Reconnect to the Internet

Use Online Help

Be Familiar with the Screens and Views

To gain an understanding of the above features, work through the **Driving Lessons** in this **Section**.

For each **Driving Lesson**, read the **Park and Read** instructions, without touching the keyboard, then work through the numbered steps of the **Manoeuvres** on the computer. Complete the **Revision Exercise(s)** at the end of the section to test your knowledge.

Driving Lesson 1 - Internet Theory

Park and Read

The **Internet** is a vast computer network, which allows users all over the world to communicate with each other. The **World Wide Web** (**www**) is not the same thing as the Internet; it is the collection of information that can be accessed via the Internet. This information is stored on the web in web sites (web pages) each of which has a unique address. The **Home Page** of a web site usually consists of an introduction to the site and often contains **hyperlinks** to other pages on that site, or to a different site on the World Wide Web.

Once connected to the Internet, it is possible to publish an individual web site. This is a simple process, as there are now software applications available which make it possible to create a publication without the need to know the Internet programming language, **HTML** (Hypertext Markup Language).

E-mail is a way of sending a message to another computer user, anywhere in the world. The message will reach its destination almost immediately. Internet users send and receive e-mail messages by using **e-mail addresses** which, like web site addresses, are unique.

Internet Explorer is an application that allows the user to access information on the World Wide Web, to publish their own web pages and to communicate with other users easily. By working through this guide, the user will be ready to access the limitless potential of electronic communication.

Communicate

There are many ways to communicate electronically; e-mail is only one route. Another very popular way of communicating, without a PC, is via **Short Message Service** (**SMS**), or text messaging between mobile phones.

In fact, online communication has opened up entire **virtual communities**. People with similar interests and hobbies can share their views on specifically dedicated web sites. These are known as **Internet forums**, where users hold discussions and post messages on specific subjects.

Social Networking Sites are used to communicate with other people and share information about yourself online. Some of the most popular sites at the moment are *MySpace*, *Facebook* and *Bebo*. These sites can combine many aspects of communication and online communities, photos and videos can be uploaded for friends to look at, as well as users being able to write blogs and send messages to each other, some messages are more like e-mails, some of the sites also contain instant messaging systems to communicate with friends also currently online.

Driving Lesson 1 - Continued

Instant messaging (**IM**),is a system where two or more users type text and it appears on screen, in real time. You always know when your contacts are online, it's a cheap way of keeping in touch and you can also transfer files. *Windows Live Messenger* is a popular instant messaging program.

Chat rooms are also popular; these are more informal and a way to meet new friends online. Chat rooms also use **instant messaging** (**IM**), in which two or more users type text and it appears on screen, in real time. Many web sites now provide the opportunity for you to play online computer games with other users, connected via the Internet.

Another way of using the PC as a communication tool is via **Voice over Internet Protocol** (**VoIP**). This works simply by using a microphone and headphones (if desired) and a third party web site's software to turn your PC into a phone. You don't pay for calls this way, although some providers do charge a small fee. Examples of VoIP providers are *Skype* and *Google Talk*.

Share

There are various ways to publish and share content such as text, photos, video and audio clips online:

Web log (**Blog**) - this is a web site where entries are posted in chronological order, like an online diary, or commentary on current affairs. Someone starts the blog and readers can leave comments on the site. A typical blog will contain text, pictures and links to other web pages. Some blogs focus on music, art or photography.

Podcast - this is where media files (audio and video) are broadcasted over the Internet. This is a convenient method of receiving music files for example, or for listening to radio programs when it suits you rather than when they are transmitted. A special format of data transfer is used to do this: **RSS feeds** (**Really Simple Syndication**). This format is also used as a way of publishing frequently updated content such as news headlines, football scores, etc. This can be sent directly to your computer or to a device such as a mobile phone. Subscribing to such a service allows you to have the latest version of any specified web page sent to you directly as it changes, without having to seek it out and refresh it.

Be cautious

These online communities can be a fantastic way of making new friends, keeping in touch and having fun. However, you must be aware that not every member of these communities may be genuine - we've all heard of identity theft, etc. With this in mind, it's important to take precautions:

- Create a private profile to keep your personal information to yourself
- Be sparing with the amount of personal information you post, because everything you do post is publicly available
- Be very wary of strangers - treat them as you would a stranger you meet on the street.

Driving Lesson 2 - Internet Explorer

Park and Read

Internet Explorer

Internet Explorer is a software application that consists of many components, designed to allow the user to explore the full potential of the Internet.

The main feature of the package is the *IE6* **web browser**, which enables the user to "surf the net." The browser facilitates searching for web sites, keeps a record of sites visited and allows favourite sites to be added to a folder for easy access.

IE6 is supplied with *Windows*, but there are other browsers available for PCs, e.g. *Mozilla Firefox*, *Safari* and *Opera*.

This guide has been written assuming that IE6 is running under Windows XP and all screen shots and options reflect this. It is however possible to run IE6 under earlier versions of Windows, in which case allowances will need to be made.

The World Wide Web is constantly being developed. In the lifetime of this guide it is likely that the content of many of the specified web sites may change from that shown here.

Driving Lesson 3 - Security on the Internet

Park and Read

Collecting information

Before using the Internet, especially at home, there are some security implications to be considered. When you access a web site, that site can also obtain information about you and can place files on your computer. This is not always as ominous as it sounds. Small text files called **cookies** are stored on your computer when you visit a web site. You can choose whether or not to allow this to happen - whether to allow some, all or none of the files to be stored. However, if you refuse all cookies you may be unable to view some web pages. As you are browsing the Internet a collection of **temporary internet files**, known as a **cache** is also stored on your computer. These speed up the display of pages that you have already visited. The main 'damage' these files (and cookies) do is take up space on your hard drive, but if desired they can be deleted.

Many web sites cannot be accessed without a user name and password; these are called **protected sites**. Sometimes you have to pay a fee up front before you can access a web site, which can then be done by entering the user name and password allocated to you. You will usually need a user name and password to shop online at supermarkets such as Sainsburys or Tesco. Indeed, all networked computers should be protected by a user name and password.

Encryption

One way of maintaining your privacy and security on the Internet is to obtain a **digital certificate** from a certification authority. This gives you a unique **private key**, which corresponds with a **public key** allocated to you by the web site. Sensitive information passing between you and the target site is **encrypted**, or scrambled using your **public key**, and can only be deciphered at the target site if they have the matching **private key**. Banks that provide an online banking service use extremely high levels of encryption for obvious reasons.

Malware

You should also be aware of potential hazards. Any annoying, hostile or intrusive software or code designed to damage a computer without the owner's knowledge is called **malware** (malicious software). Some files downloaded from the Internet contain **viruses** and other threats, which are programs intended to cause harm to your computer. A specific type of threat is a **worm**; this is a self replicating program, which sends copies of itself to linked computers and therefore uses a great deal of bandwidth. Another threat is a **Trojan horse**, which appears to do one thing, but in reality does another, e.g. installs a program. Viruses can be transmitted in this way, but neither a worm nor a Trojan horse is a virus. **Spyware** is software that is installed without your knowledge. It can monitor your behaviour and collect various types of personal information; it can also change your computer settings.

Driving Lesson 3 - Continued

Anti-virus software

Viruses are often attached to e-mail messages. It is vital to have anti-virus software installed and equally important to keep it updated on a weekly basis at least. It is also possible to install a **firewall**. This is a program that protects your computer from any unauthorised access or intrusion from outside, such as someone trying to access the hard drive to obtain passwords, etc. It is advisable to install a firewall if you have a broadband (always on) connection.

There are many forms of anti-virus software to counter these threats and most PCs have it installed when bought. However, it's extremely important to update it at least on a weekly basis. New threats are developing all the time. You must also perform scans for viruses on a regular basis.

Secure shopping

If you decide to do some shopping on the Internet, make sure you pay using a **secure server**. These web pages can be identified by a small padlock symbol  on the **Status Bar** and **https** at the beginning of the address. Unfortunately, there is a small risk of credit card fraud when paying for goods online, but it must be stressed that the risk is really no greater than giving your credit card details to someone in a shop or over the telephone. There are great advantages to shopping online: you don't have to go out and jostle your way through crowds or find city centre parking and it is possible to buy almost anything you can think of from all over the world.

Parental control

There is an unbelievable amount of data on the world wide web. There are sites representing every aspect of human life. It follows then, that there may be content which is offensive to even the most broad-minded person. Indeed, there is some content placed on the web for the sole purpose of being offensive.

Whilst the average person may consider the occasional inadvertent view of offensive material an acceptable price to pay for unrestricted access to the web, there are situations where all possible steps should be taken to prevent this, particularly in the case of access by children. At the time of writing there are no restrictions of any kind built into the Internet, anyone can access anything. There have also been cases of harassment, bullying and, even worse, predators prowling the web to find unsupervised children online. There are, however, external methods of imposing control. Parents can help by physically supervising their children's online time; they can also restrict their browsing, supervise game playing and restrict time spent on the Internet.

If physical supervision is not always possible, Internet browsers (and some firewalls) include content filters, which can allow or restrict access based on a rating system or by individual site. Commercial software is available which will restrict access to sites based on content and by individual site. This software often includes the ability to monitor and restrict chat room access, currently an increasing area of concern.

Driving Lesson 3 - Continued

Manoeuvres

1. Select **Start | Control Panel** and open **Internet Options**. If you are in **Category** view select the **Network and Internet Connections** category first.

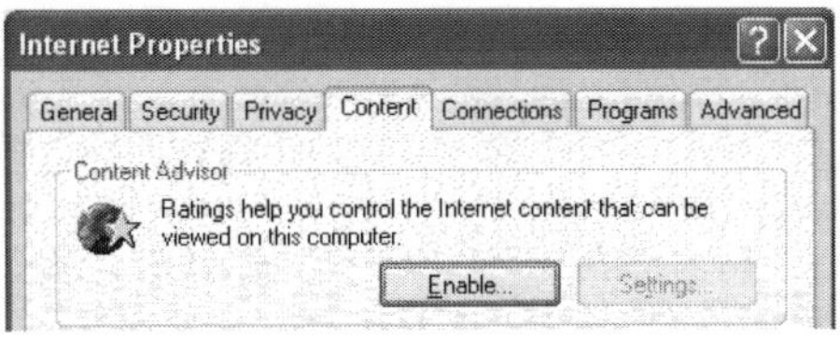

2. Select the **Content** tab of the **Internet Properties** dialog box and look at the buttons in the **Content Advisor** area.

*If **Content Advisor** is currently enabled, there will be a **Disable** button rather than an **Enable** button. If **Content Advisor** has never been activated, the **Settings** button will be unavailable.*

3. To change the **Content Advisor** settings when it has not yet been activated, click **Enable**. If it has been activated, click **Settings**, enter the **Supervisor** password if prompted and click **OK**.

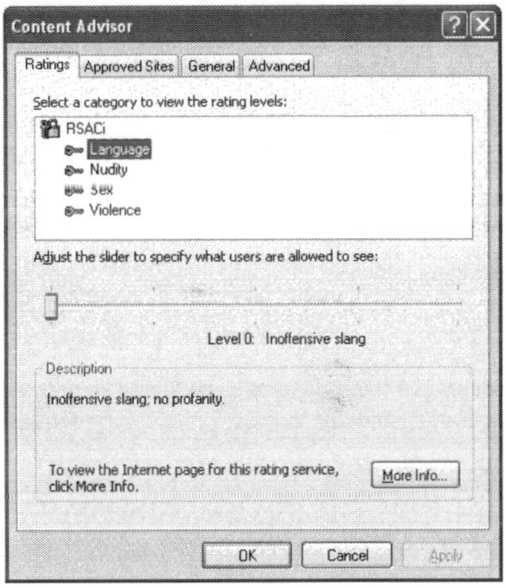

4. Click on each **Category** and set the **slider** to the required level of access.
5. Click the **Approved Sites** tab and enter addresses (URLs) of specific sites that can **Always** be viewed or **Never** be viewed.
6. Click the **General** tab. There is an option to allow users to see any site that does not have a rating. If this is not selected, only sites with the required ratings can be viewed.
7. There is also a button here to allow the **Supervisor password** to be changed (the original password must be known). Setting a password here for the first time will activate the system. The password is case sensitive.
8. Click **Cancel** to ignore any changes, including activation.

*Only click **OK** to accept the settings and possibly activate the system if you are sure that is what you want. Once activated, the **Content Advisor** system can only be enabled, disabled or amended by using the password. The password will always be required.*

9. Close the **Internet Properties** dialog box and the **Control Panel** window.

Driving Lesson 4 - Connecting to the Internet

Park and Read

Before connecting to the Internet, the user must either have a **broadband** (always on) connection, or a **dial-up** connection (see next driving lesson) available.

Your broadband connection can be supplied using a telephone line, cable or satellite. Sometimes there will be a device (router) that must be switched on to make the connection, sometimes it will be permanently available. Connection between your computer and the broadband system can use cables or be wireless.

On a network, the internet connection will probably be made via the server and made available automatically at all networked computers.

It is also necessary to subscribe to an **Internet Service Provider (ISP)**. They handle all the information to and from your computer and provide the connection service between your computer and the rest of the Internet. They will normally also supply an **e-mail address**.

Manoeuvres

1. Select 

from the *Windows* **Desktop** and select **All Programs | Internet Explorer** (then possibly **Internet Explorer** again, depending on the computer's setup). If there is not a current connection, the **Dial-up Connection** dialog box will be displayed.

2. The *Internet Explorer* window will be displayed. If the connection to the Internet is active the window will show a web page.

If the connection to the Internet is not active for any reason, an appropriate message will be displayed.

3. The default starting web page shown whenever an Internet connection is first made, is known as your **Home Page**. This guide displays the *Microsoft* site, **msn.com**, as the **Home Page** but it will affect the following driving lessons if your Home page is different. Leave the default starting web page open.

It is possible to change your Home Page at any time. If you want to change your Home Page, go to Driving Lesson 28 and perform steps 1-3, substituting the site of your choice for ***www.altavista.com****.*

Driving Lesson 5 - Dial Up Connection

Park and Read

If there is no broadband connection available, it is possible to have a dial-up connection to the Internet. This usually involves having a **modem** installed or connected to the computer; this is a device that converts signals from the computer into signals that can travel through a phone line. Using a dial-up connection takes over exclusive use of a telephone line whilst connected. Normal voice calls will not be possible on that line while the Internet is being used.

This driving lesson should only be read if using a dial up connection.

Manoeuvres

1. Select 

from the *Windows* **Desktop** select **All Programs | Internet Explorer**. If there is not a current connection, the **Dial-up Connection** dialog box will be displayed.

Depending on the settings on the computer, the connection may be dialled automatically.

2. The default **Connect to** location will be displayed. The **User name** and **Password** may already be present, as in the diagram. If not, when the **Dial-up Connection** dialog box is displayed, enter the relevant **User name** and **Password**. Click on **Connect**.

*Different systems may have different **Dial-up Connection** dialog boxes.*

3. The *Internet Explorer* window will be displayed showing your **Home Page** web site as before.

*The connection may be lost for technical reasons or if it has been inactive for a certain length of time. The **Dial-up Connection** dialog box will be displayed again.*

Driving Lesson 6 - Browser Help

Park and Read

Internet Explorer contains an online **Help** facility that may assist when certain problems are experienced.

Manoeuvres

1. The default **Home Page** (**msn.com**) is shown on the screen. This will be explained in the next few Driving Lessons.

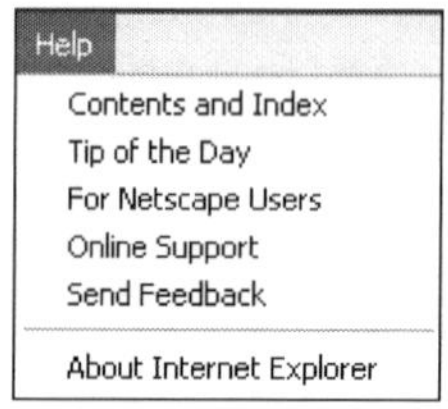

2. To find out more about **Help**, click on **Help** on the **Menu Bar** at the top of the screen. A further list of choices appears.
3. Select **Contents and Index**. The **Help** Window is displayed. This has a tabbed pane on the left and a content area on the right.
4. Click on the **Contents** tab. This groups all **Help** topics into sections like the chapters in a book.
5. Click on any section (book) to open it and display a list of topics. Click on any topic to display help text for that topic in the right of the window.
6. Click on the **Index** tab. A list of indexed keywords is displayed. Type **virus** in the box at the top to display the relevant part of the list. Click on the entry from the list and click **Display**.

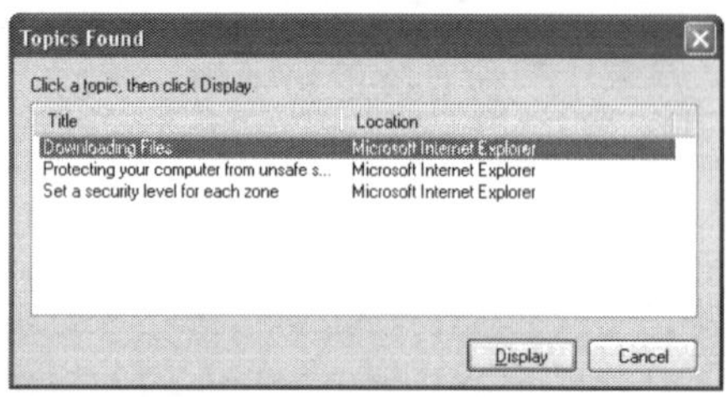

7. There may be a further choice of topics presented. Select one from the list and click **Display**. The relevant help text will be displayed on the right.
8. Click on the **Search** tab. Type **virus** in the box at the top and click **List Topics**. A list of topics which contain the search word is displayed. Select an entry from the list and click **Display** to display the relevant help text.
9. Click the **Close** button, ☒, at the top right corner of the **Help** window to close it.

*The **Online Support** option from the **Help** menu will open the **Microsoft Help and Support** web page with links to a variety of topics. Using web pages is covered in later exercises in this guide.*

Driving Lesson 7 - Internet Explorer Screen

Park and Read

Once the user has made the connection to the Internet, the designated **Home Page** will appear. In this guide we assume it is the **Microsoft** site, **msn.com**.

Manoeuvres

1. Look at the screen. It may look slightly different to the picture below, because the *Microsoft* web pages are constantly changing.

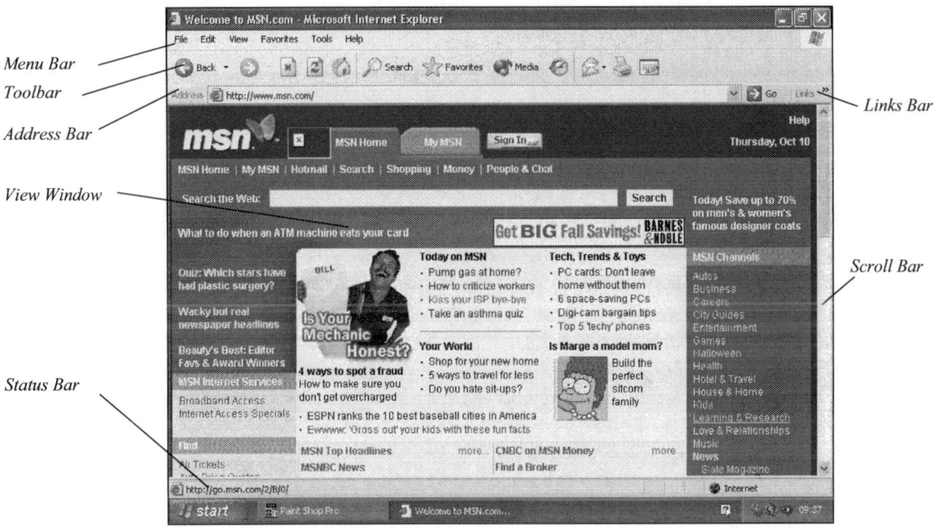

The home page consists of the:

Menu Bar	containing a variety of drop down commands from which to make a selection.
Toolbar	containing a series of icons which perform the most common commands.
Address Bar	displaying the address of the web site being viewed.
Links Bar	which provides a quick way of getting to another web page.
View window	which displays the actual web page.
Status Bar	which shows the user exactly what *Explorer* is doing.
Scroll Bar	at the far right of the screen, which allows the user to move up and down the page.

Driving Lesson 8 - Views

Park and Read

Some functions within *Internet Explorer* change the view of the screen by opening an area on the left of the screen known as the **Explorer Bar**, from which the function is then controlled. For example, the **Search** button opens an **Explorer Bar** which allows the various search parameters and options to be defined. The bar is then referred to as the **Search Bar**. Other functions which open **Explorer Bars** include **Favorites** and **History**.

Full Screen View can be selected to view more of the web page by suppressing all toolbars except the **Standard** toolbar.

Manoeuvres

1. With your default **Home Page** (**msn.com**) on the screen, click the **Search** button, , to view the **Search Bar** at the left of the screen.
2. Click on the **Search** button again to remove the **Search Bar**.
3. Click the **Favorites** button, , to display the **Favorites Bar**.
4. Click the **History** button, . The **Favorites Bar** is closed and the **History Bar** appears, showing the pages that have been visited recently. By default, *Explorer* keeps a record of the sites visited within the past 20 days, although this period may have been altered.
5. Close the **History Bar** by clicking the **History** button again or the **Close** button, , at the top right of the **History Bar**.

*The **Search** and **Favorites** features will be discussed in greater detail later. Pages listed in the **History** or **Favorites** can be displayed by clicking on them.*

6. The toolbar display can also be modified. Select **View | Toolbars**. Those toolbars currently displayed have a tick next to them. Click on **Address Bar** to hide this toolbar.
7. To replace the toolbar, select **View | Toolbars | Address Bar**.

***View | Toolbars | Customize** has a **Text options** box which alters the appearance of toolbars. This guide uses the **Selective text on right** option.*

8. Select **View | Full Screen** from the menu.
9. To return to the normal view, click the **Restore** button, , in the top right corner of the screen and leave the **Home Page** open.

*The <**F11**> key can be used to toggle between **Full Screen** and normal view.*

Driving Lesson 9 - Framed Web Pages

Park and Read

Some web sites have **framed** pages, consisting of a **Navigation panel** and a **View panel**. These pages work in a similar way to *Windows Explorer*, that is, selecting an option in the Navigation panel will display its contents in the View panel. The framed page often has scroll bars as navigation aids.

The advantage of framed web pages is that the user can see the contents of a web site at a glance. However, the downside is that these sites can sometimes be difficult to exit.

Manoeuvres

1. Click in the **Address Bar** of the *Explorer* window and type **www.ciatraining.co.uk/downloads**, then press <**Enter**>. This is a **framed** page: a list of navigation hyperlinks is at the left of the screen. When one of the links is clicked, a new page will be shown at the right of the screen.

Web addresses will be covered in more detail in Driving Lesson 15.

2. Click on the **Images** text at the left. This is a hyperlink (like the rest of the bulleted list). Notice how the information at the right of the screen changes.
3. Read the information.
4. There is a further hyperlink underneath the images. Click on the word **here** under the smallest banana. Another new page is displayed.
5. Notice how the navigation hyperlinks are always visible at the left of the screen.
6. Click on the **Home Page** text hyperlink to move to the **Home Page** for the site.

*The **Back** button,* 

, can be used to move back through the pages (see Driving Lesson 14).

*The **Home** button,* *, can be used to exit a complex framed web site.*

7. Click on the  button to display your default **Home Page**.

Driving Lesson 10 - Closing the Browser

Park and Read

To end the current browsing session, the web browser must be closed. With a dial up connection, make sure the connection is also terminated, if you are not prompted to disconnect automatically.

Manoeuvres

1. Click the **Close** button, , on the **Menu Bar** at the top right corner of the screen.

*Alternatively, select **File | Close** from the menu.*

2. If you have a dial up connection the **Auto Disconnect** dialog box should appear.

3. Select **Disconnect Now** to end the current session. If the **Auto Disconnect** dialog box does not appear, move to step 5.

4. Reconnect to the Internet, by clicking on the button on the **Taskbar** or **Desktop**, or selecting **Start | All Programs**, etc.

5. The icon , is always visible on the **Taskbar** when the computer is connected to the Internet. Click on to display a **Connected to** dialog box showing status details of the current connection.

6. Click **Disconnect** to end the current session. Confirm that the has disappeared. Always ensure that this icon is not displayed to signify disconnection.

7. Reconnect to the Internet.

Driving Lesson 11 - Revision

This covers the features introduced in this section. Try not to refer to the preceding Driving Lessons while completing it.

1. What does **www** stand for?
2. What is the main programming language used on the Internet?
3. What must you have before attempting to connect to the Internet?
4. Use online help to find out about *Microsoft* **Product Updates**.
5. Which buttons can be used to change the view of the screen?
6. Why are framed web pages used?
7. Disconnect from the Internet.

Check the answers at the back of the guide.

If you experienced any difficulty completing the Revision, refer back to the Driving Lessons in this section. Then redo the Revision.

Driving Lesson 12 - Revision

This covers the features introduced in this section. Try not to refer to the preceding Driving Lessons while completing it.

1. Connect to the Internet.
2. What is the Internet?
3. How is the **World Wide Web** different from the Internet?
4. What are **cookies**?
5. What does **encrypted** mean?
6. What is a **firewall**?
7. How can you determine if a server is secure before attempting to pay for goods online using a credit card?

Check the answers at the back of the guide.

If you experienced any difficulty completing the Revision, refer back to the Driving Lessons in this section. Then redo the Revision.

Once you are confident with the features, complete the Record of Achievement Matrix referring to the section at the end of the guide. Only when competent move on to the next Section.

Section 2 Navigation

By the end of this Section you should be able to:

Use Hyperlinks

Move Backward and Forward through a Web Site

Use Web Addresses

Store and Organise Bookmarks

Use the History Feature

Stop and Refresh Downloads

To gain an understanding of the above features, work through the **Driving Lessons** in this **Section**.

For each **Driving Lesson**, read the **Park and Read** instructions, without touching the keyboard, then work through the numbered steps of the **Manoeuvres** on the computer. Complete the **Revision Exercise(s)** at the end of the section to test your knowledge.

Driving Lesson 13 - Using Hyperlinks

Park and Read

Most web sites contain **hyperlinks**. These are pieces of coloured text, pictures or buttons which, when activated, immediately take the user to a different site, or a different page within the current site.

There is no limit to the number of hyperlinks a web site can have. It is because any site can be linked to many other related sites, each one of which in turn will be linked to many more, that led to the idea of a huge 'web' of information (the world wide web). This interconnected mass of information can be browsed relatively simply by choosing a trail of hyperlinks from one site to another.

The advantage of using hyperlinks to navigate within the pages of a single site is that they make it much more interesting and user-friendly.

Manoeuvres

1. Connect to the Internet, if you are not already connected.
2. Enter **www.ciatraining.co.uk/downloads** in the **Address Bar** and press <**Enter**> or click the **Go** button, .

*These pages are part of the **CiA Training Ltd** web site and are only accessed by entering the above address fully and correctly.*

3. Click on the link **Hyperlinks** in the left frame of the screen. A new page is displayed in the right frame. Read the information that is displayed.

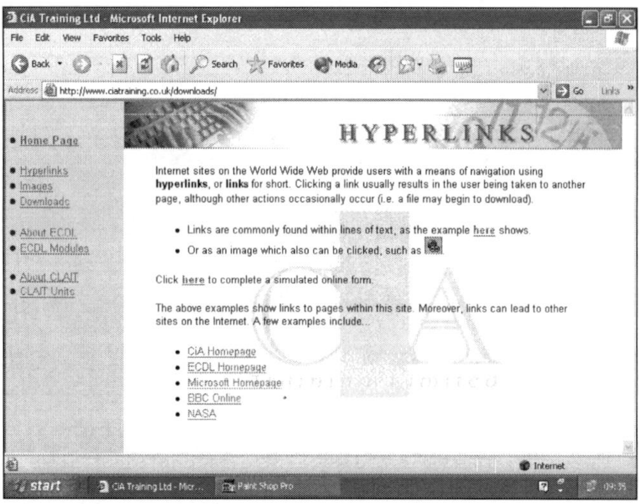

Driving Lesson 13 - Continued

This site is an example of framed web pages. The navigation pane on the left remains constant and contains links to the other pages of the site. These content pages are displayed in the frame on the right as they are selected.

4. Click the **About ECDL** hyperlink in the left frame.
5. When the new page is displayed, read through the text then click the **ECDL Modules** hyperlink at the left to display a new page.
6. Hyperlinks can be used to open a web page in a new window. Right click on the **Downloads** link in the left frame of the page.
7. From the shortcut menu, select **Open in New Window**. A smaller window opens containing the new web page.
8. Click its **Close** button to remove the window.
9. To demonstrate a hyperlink to a new site, click on **Hyperlinks** in the left frame of the screen. When the new page is displayed in the right frame, click on the **NASA** link.
10. The **NASA** site is displayed in a new window because of the way that the hyperlink has been programmed. Maximise the new window, then click its **Close** button to remove it.
11. Click  to return to the your default **Home Page**.

Driving Lesson 14 - Back and Forward Buttons

Park and Read

Navigating between web pages/sites is made easy by using the **Back**,  and **Forward**, 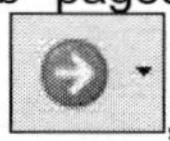, buttons on the **Toolbar**. *Explorer* records the order in which pages are viewed. The **Back** button moves back through the pages until the first page viewed is reached. The **Forward** button moves forward until the most recently viewed page is reached. Clicking the arrow to the right of each button displays a drop down list of all sites visited before or after the current one. Any site can be selected from the list.

Manoeuvres

1. With your default **Home Page** still being viewed, click the **Back** button, . The screen displays the last page visited.
2. Repeat this action until the button becomes ghosted (pale grey). This means that the first page viewed in this session has been reached.
3. Now click the **Forward** button, 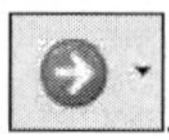. *Explorer* will move forward to the next page in the sequence.
4. Repeat step 3 to move forward through the pages until the **Forward** button is ghosted. This indicates that the most recent page is displayed and it is not possible to go further forward.
5. Click the small arrow to the right of the **Back** button to reveal a drop down list of all previous sites.
6. Click any one to go to it directly.
7. If your default **Home Page** is not displayed, click  to return to it and leave it open.

Driving Lesson 15 - Using Web Addresses

Park and Read

The quickest and easiest way of visiting a web site is by entering its **address**, or **URL (Uniform Resource Locator)**, in the **Address Bar**. It is important to ensure that the exact address is entered. Because of the sheer volume of sites on the World Wide Web, it would be almost impossible to locate the required site without a complete address, unless it is a large multinational company.

A **protocol** is a language that enables computers to speak to one another. All web sites use the protocol **http** (**Hypertext Transfer Protocol**). *Internet Explorer* automatically enters (**http://**), to start the web address. The next part of the address is the **domain name** and is broken up into several segments, separated by periods. The first is usually **www** (**World Wide Web**) then a name that often indicates the name of the organisation who owns the site, then one or more segments indicating the kind of organisation or the country where the server is located, e.g. **com**, **co.uk**, **gov**, etc. that owns the server. Each country has a different last segment of the domain name, e.g. in Australia it is **au** and in Germany it is **de**, so some web addresses will end with these letters.

Every web site has a **Home Page**; this is the first page to appear when the site is opened. The Home Page usually consists of a welcome and/or introduction to the site and links to other pages within it. Note the difference from your default **Home Page**, which is the page loaded by the **Browser** when it starts or when you press the **Home** button.

Manoeuvres

1. Click in the **Address Bar** and enter the following address: **www.ciatraining.co.uk** (the address of our main web site) then press <**Enter**> or click Go.

*The drop down list on the **Address Bar** can be used to access recently visited sites. Just click on the arrow and select an address from the list.*

2. Browse the details of the **CiA** site, then click the **Home** button, , to return to the your default **Home Page**.

3. In the **Address Bar** type in **www.disney.com** and press <**Enter**>.

*If the site required is that of a large company, the address you enter may be converted into one more suitable or current, such as **www.home.disney.co.uk**.*

4. After viewing the details of the **Disney** site, return to your default **Home Page** by clicking the **Home** button.

Driving Lesson 16 - Bookmarks

Park and Read

After using *Internet Explorer* to browse the web, it is likely that the user will have visited some sites that they would like to revisit on a regular basis. *Explorer*'s **Favorites** feature provides a quick and hassle free way of doing just that! In a few easy steps favourite sites can be added to a list which, when clicked on, will take the user directly to that site. This is known as **bookmarking** a web page.

Once a list of bookmarks has been created, it can be displayed by clicking the **Favorites** button. Any site from the list can then be visited by a click of the mouse.

A subscription to a favourite site can be set up, so that *Explorer* will inform the user if any updates have taken place since their last visit (by showing a red star on its icon within the **Favorites** list). By customising the **Favorites** list, a user can choose to be notified of updates via e-mail.

Manoeuvres

1. Click on the drop down arrow of the **Address Bar** and select the **Disney** home page from the list.

2. Browse the site, then use the 

button to return to the **Disney** home page.

3. When the **Disney** home page is displayed, click 

to display the list of current favourites in the **Favorites Bar**. The contents of the list will vary depending on which pages have already been selected.

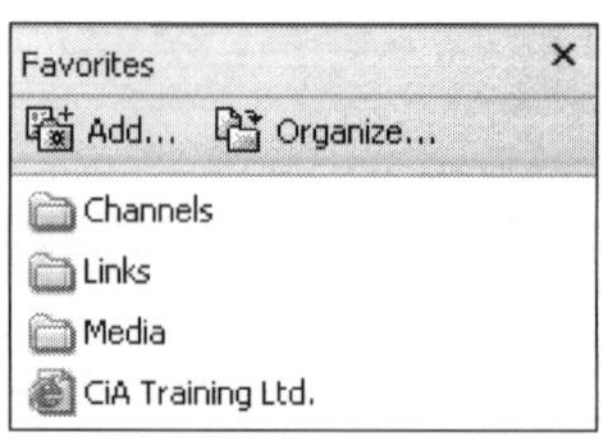

4. To add a bookmark, click the **Add** button, 

. The **Add Favorite** dialog box is displayed.

5. Edit the text in the **Name** field to just **Disney Online**.

Driving Lesson 16 - Continued

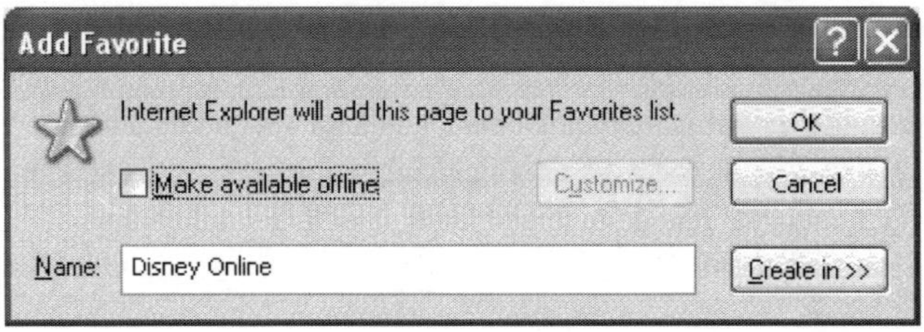

*Alternatively, selecting the command **Favorites | Add to Favorites** from the **Menu Bar** will display the dialog box without having the **Favourites Bar** open.*

6. Click **OK** to add the **Disney** page to your list of favourites.
7. Click on the **Home** button, , then enter the address **www.ciatraining.co.uk** in the **Address Bar**. Now press <**Enter**>.
8. Browse the site, then use the  button to return to the **CiA** home page.
9. When the **CiA** home page appears, repeat steps **4** and **6** to add it to your list of favourites, use the name **CIA**.
10. Click on the **Home** button, , then enter **www.nasa.gov** in the **Address Bar**. Press <**Enter**>.
11. Browse the **NASA** site, then return to its home page using the  button.
12. When the **NASA** home page is displayed, repeat steps **4** and **6** to add it to your list of favourites, use the name **NASA**.
13. Return to your default **Home Page** by clicking . Several sites have now been added to your bookmarks.
14. To display a bookmarked site, select **Disney Online** from the entries listed in the **Favorites Bar** to go directly to that site.
15. Return immediately to your default **Home Page** using the  button.

Driving Lesson 17 - Organising Bookmarks

Park and Read

Once a **Favorites** list has been created, *Internet Explorer* allows the user to manage these links in a similar way to *Windows Explorer* manages files. Favourites can be moved, renamed or deleted, folders and keyboard shortcuts can be created.

Manoeuvres

1. If necessary, click the **Favorites** button to display the **Favorites Bar**.
2. Select the **Organize** button, 

. The **Organize Favorites** dialog box is displayed (the contents may be slightly different to the diagram).

*Alternatively, select the command **Favorites** | **Organize Favorites**.*

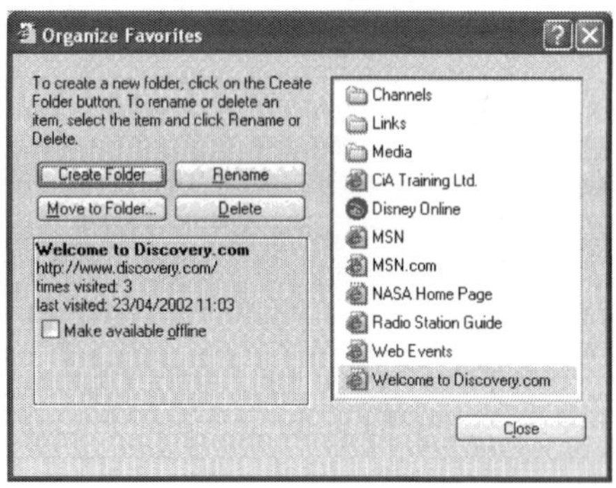

3. Click the **Create Folder** button at the top of the dialog box and name the new folder **Entertainment**. Press <**Enter**>.
4. Scroll the list of pages and select the **Disney Online** page. Click on the **Move to Folder** button.
5. Select the newly created folder, **Entertainment**, then click **OK**. The **Disney** link has been moved to the new folder.
6. Select the **NASA** page from the **Favorites** list and click **Rename**.
7. Change the name of the entry to **Space Exploration**, then press <**Enter**>.
8. Select the **CIA** link and click **Delete** to display the prompt **Are you sure you want to send ... to the Recycle Bin?**, Selecting **Yes** would remove the page from the favourites list but for now click **No** to retain the entry.

*To delete a folder, just select it before clicking <**Delete**>.*

9. Rename the **CIA** entry **CIA Training Ltd**.
10. Click **Close**, but leave your default **Home Page** open.

Driving Lesson 18 - The Links Bar

Park and Read

The **Favorites Bar** provides quick access to the user's list of bookmarks. Favourite sites can also be added to the **Links** toolbar, which is the quickest way to access these sites, although it does have limited space.

Manoeuvres

1. If the **Favorites Bar** is not in view, click the **Favorites** button, 

, to display it.

2. The **CIA** site is to be added to the **Links** toolbar. Move the mouse over the **CIA Training Ltd** page in the **Favorites Bar**.

3. Hold the button down and drag the **CIA** link to the **Links Bar**, (to the right of the **Address Bar**), then release the mouse.

*By default the **Links Bar** is located at the right of the **Address Bar** and is accessed as a drop down list by clicking on the chevrons. It can however be expanded to a full toolbar with the entries shown as icons.*

4. To add the **Disney** site to the **Links Bar** click the **Entertainment** folder in the **Favorites Bar** to open it. Repeat steps **2** and **3** for the **Disney** site.

5. The **Disney** site was added to **Links** in error. If necessary click the chevrons to the right of the **Links Bar** to display the list of sites.

6. Right click on the **Disney** site address in the list (or the icon on the toolbar) and select **Delete** from the shortcut menu.

7. A dialog box appears asking for confirmation that it is to be removed and sent to the recycle bin. Click **Yes**.

8. Display the **Organize Favorites** dialog box and delete the **Entertainment** folder and the **CIA Training Ltd** entry from the **Links** folder (double click the **Links** folder to open it if necessary).

9. Close the dialog box then close the **Favorites Bar** by clicking its **Close** button, 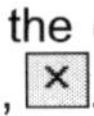.

10. Leave your default **Home Page** open for the next Driving Lesson.

Driving Lesson 19 - Browsing History

Park and Read

As you are browsing, a record is kept of all the web pages visited. This is known as a **browsing history**. The **Address Bar** can be used to return to previously visited pages. The **History Bar** also allows quick and easy access to previously visited web sites. By default *Explorer* keeps a record of the sites visited within the past 20 days, although this period can be altered to suit the user's personal requirements. It is also possible to clear this history at any time.

Manoeuvres

1. Click the drop down arrow at the right of the **Address Bar**, . Notice how the recently visited pages are listed.
2. Click on the **Disney** address, 

. You are taken straight to the Disney site.
3. Now use the **Address Bar** list to go to the **NASA** page.
4. Click the **History** button, 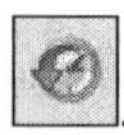. The **History Bar** appears at the left of the screen. The sites visited in the previous exercises should be present, along with any sites viewed by other users within the default period.

*The **History Bar** can also be displayed by selecting the command **View | Explorer Bar | History**.*

5. Click on **View** from the **History Bar** and make sure that the view selected from the drop down options is **By Order Visited Today**.

*In some views of the **History Bar** the pages visited are all grouped by site into folders. The folders must be opened to see the individual pages.*

6. Select the **Disney** site from the **History Bar** by clicking on it. Close the **History Bar** by clicking the **Close** button, , within the bar.
7. Within this site, select **View | Explorer Bar | History** and the **History Bar** will be displayed.
8. Choose to visit the **NASA** site by clicking on it.

Driving Lesson 19 - Continued

9. Select **Tools | Internet Options**, then the **General** tab from the **Internet Options** dialog box.

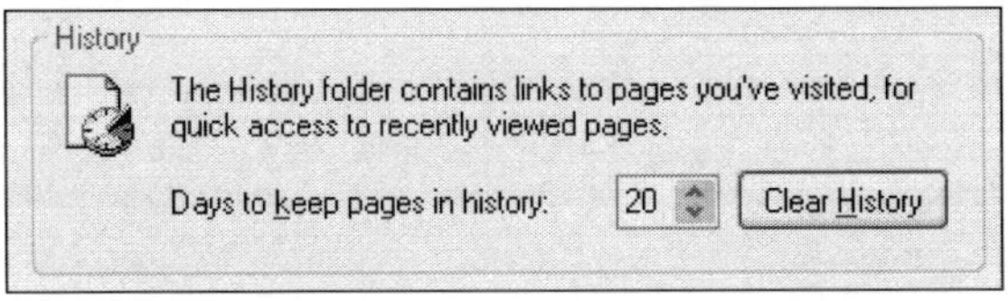

10. To delete the browsing history, click the **Clear History** button.

11. At the confirmation prompt **Are you sure you want Windows to delete your History of visited web sites?**, click **Yes**.

To delete part of the browsing history, reduce the number in ***Days to keep pages in History*** *and click* ***OK****. Press <**F5**> to refresh the settings.*

12. Click **OK** to close the dialog box.

13. Look at the **History Bar** again – none of the web sites visited should be there.

It is possible, due to the configuration of IE6 or the presence of other programs, that the ***History*** *entries are not completely cleared by this process. If this occurs consult your IT administrator or a technical expert.*

14. Close the **History Bar**. Check the **Address Bar** drop down list. This has also been cleared.

15. Click **Home**, , to return to your default **Home Page**.

Driving Lesson 20 - Stop and Refresh Downloads

Park and Read

When a web page is opened, it automatically begins to **download**. This can often take a long time, for example, if there are a lot of graphics. The download can be stopped, if necessary. The **Refresh** feature will start the download again. Some web sites are being constantly changed or updated, even as they are viewed. **Refresh** can also ensure that the most up to date version of the site is being viewed.

Manoeuvres

1. Enter the web address **www.nationalgeographic.com** in the **Address Bar** and press <**Enter**>.

2. As the graphics are being downloaded, click the **Stop** button, , on the toolbar. The download will halt.

3. Click the **Refresh** button, . The downloading begins again.

4. Use the **Favorites** button, , to visit the **NASA** site (**Space Exploration**).

5. After viewing the site, use to return to the **nationalgeographic** site. The download begins automatically, because you have re-entered the site.

6. **Refresh** can be useful when viewing some webcams (live images from cameras which are displayed on a web page). Visit the site **www.bbc.co.uk/england/webcams/** which features webcam displays from around the country.

7. Select a topic, e.g. **Traffic**, and click on any webcam display where there may be some visible activity, e.g. **Tyne Tunnel**.

8. A new image is transmitted every few minutes. Click **Refresh**, , every minute or so to see the most recent image when it becomes available.

*There are webcams on many other sites, e.g. **earthcam.com**. Note that some webcams are live video streams and therefore do not need refreshing.*

9. Click to return to your default **Home Page**.

Driving Lesson 21 - Revision

This covers the features introduced in this section. Try not to refer to the preceding Driving Lessons while completing it.

1. Type the address **www.sainsburys.com** in the **Address Bar**.
2. Use hyperlinks to view topics of interest to you.
3. Use the **Back** button, , to return to the **Sainsbury's** home page.
4. Bookmark the page.
5. Now visit the **CNN** home page (**www.cnn.com**).
6. Bookmark the home page.
7. Create a folder called **News** and move the **CNN** link into it.
8. Navigate the **CNN** site using hyperlinks,  and 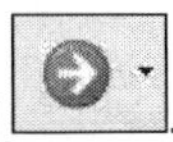.
9. The **CNN** home page is updated hourly. **Refresh** the page to see if it has changed.
10. Remove the **Sainsburys** and **Space Exploration** entries from the **Favorites** list.
11. Delete the folder **News** and all its contents.
12. Return to your default **Home Page**.

If you experienced any difficulty completing the Revision, refer back to the Driving Lessons in this section. Then redo the Revision.

Driving Lesson 22 - Revision

This covers the features introduced in this section. Try not to refer to the preceding Driving Lessons while completing it.

1. Go to **www.bbc.co.uk**.
2. Use some of the hyperlinks to browse the site.
3. Go to your default **Home Page**.
4. Use the **Address Bar** list to visit the **BBC** page.
5. Display the **History Bar**.
6. Use it to visit any site seen earlier today.
7. Close the **History Bar**.
8. Clear the browsing history.

If you experienced any difficulty completing the Revision, refer back to the Driving Lessons in this section. Then redo the Revision.

Once you are confident with the features, complete the Record of Achievement Matrix referring to the section at the end of the guide. Only when competent move on to the next Section.

Section 3
Browsing the Web

By the end of this Section you should be able to:

Browse the Web using Search Engines

Use Subject Directories

Use the Search Bar

Find Text on a Page

To gain an understanding of the above features, work through the **Driving Lessons** in this **Section**.

For each **Driving Lesson**, read the **Park and Read** instructions, without touching the keyboard, then work through the numbered steps of the **Manoeuvres** on the computer. Complete the **Revision Exercise(s)** at the end of the section to test your knowledge.

Driving Lesson 23 - Search Engines

Park and Read

A **search engine** is a facility connected to a vast database. Once the user has entered key words, the search engine will select every site on its database containing those words.

Some search engines are:

Google	**www.google.co.uk**
Yahoo	**www.yahoo.co.uk**
Lycos	**www.lycos.co.uk**
AltaVista	**www.altavista.com**

But there are many others available and new ones are appearing all the time. *Google* is possibly the most popular at time of writing. Each search engine has a **search box**, where the user enters details of the subject they want to find.

Manoeuvres

1. Enter **www.yahoo.co.uk** in the **Address Bar**. Press <**Enter**> and the **Yahoo** search engine is launched.
2. In the **search box**, enter the following search: **shark**.
3. There is an option where to search - select **UK only**.

As sites are frequently updated, the screen may look slightly different to the one above.

4. Click on the **Web Search** button to the right of the box. If there is a security warning about submitting information, click **Yes** to continue but be aware of the implications of the message.
5. After a few seconds **Yahoo** will retrieve every site on its database which contains this word. The number of matches is usually displayed at the top of the list of sites.
6. Some commercially sponsored sites may be listed first or in a panel on the right. Select the first 'real' Web site match and browse the site.
7. Click the **Back** button until the **Yahoo** home page is displayed again.
8. With **Shark** still in the search box, click **Images**. Links to images related to sharks will be listed.
9. Return to your default **Home Page** by clicking the **Home** button.

Driving Lesson 24 - Search Criteria

Park and Read

The previous Driving Lesson demonstrates a common problem encountered by Internet users: a search can produce hundreds of thousands of **"hits"**, not all of them relevant to the intended subject. It is possible to narrow the search considerably by using certain criteria.

Specify the language	Use the **Language** drop down list in the **search box**.
Use lowercase text	This will search for lower **and** uppercase words.
Include key words	Enter a **+** before the key word, e.g. **films + Scorcese**.
Exclude words	Enter a **-** before an unwanted word, e.g. **french + wine - champagne**.
Use phrases	In speech marks, for words which always go together, e.g. **"Tom and Jerry"** or **"The Battle of Hastings"** to specify an exact phrase.

Manoeuvres

1. Go to the **AltaVista** search engine by entering the address **www.altavista.com** in the **Address Bar**. Press <**Enter**>.

2. You want to find a recipe for chicken satay. Narrow the search by selecting the options for **UK** sites in **English** language, if not already selected.

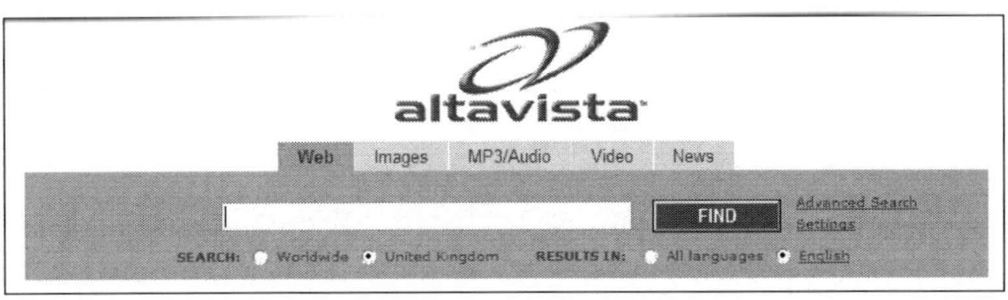

3. In the **Search** box, type **recipe chinese** then click **Find**.

4. Scroll down the page. The number of pages found that match the search should be displayed. A large number of matches will be found!

5. Click  to return to **AltaVista's** home page.

Driving Lesson 24 - Continued

6. In some search engines a **+** criteria will narrow down a search by insisting that the following word is included in the page. Enter **recipe +satay +chinese** in the search box (make sure there are spaces before the **+** signs). Click **Find**. There should now be fewer matches.

7. Try this search: **"chicken satay"** (include speech marks). The search will now only find pages where these words occur together in a phrase, but will no longer be restricted to those sites containing the word '**chinese**'.

8. Select a recipe from the list by clicking on its hyperlink. Read the recipe, then return to the **AltaVista** home page by clicking .

9. To see an example of narrowing a search, try to find web sites about **sea angling**. Start by searching for **angling**. Take note of the number of matches, that is the number of pages that contain the word '**angling**'. There should be a vast number.

10. Now search for pages containing the two words **sea angling**. The two words can be anywhere on the page. There may still be several thousand but the number should be less than before.

11. Next search for the phrase "**sea angling**". Use speech marks around the phrase. Now the words must occur together. The number of matches will be further reduced.

12. Now enter your name, separated by a **+** in the search box, e.g. **Amanda + Laughton**, and press **Find**. Make a note of the number of matches found.

13. Now enter your name in speech marks, e.g. **"Amanda Laughton"**. The number of matches should have reduced.

*Explorer includes the **Autosearch** function - a quicker, simple to use way of retrieving matches. It is possible to find the web site of a large multinational company, **Esso**, for example, by entering their name in the **Address Bar**, then pressing <**Enter**>.*

14. You can also narrow searches by various means. From the **AltaVista** home page, click **Advanced Search**.

Notice how the area at the top allows you to include or exclude specific words or phrases.

Driving Lesson 24 - Continued

15. Your task is to find any *Word* document, created between 1st January 2007 and the current date, containing a recipe for blueberry muffins. Complete the details as below; remember to select the **Worldwide** option.

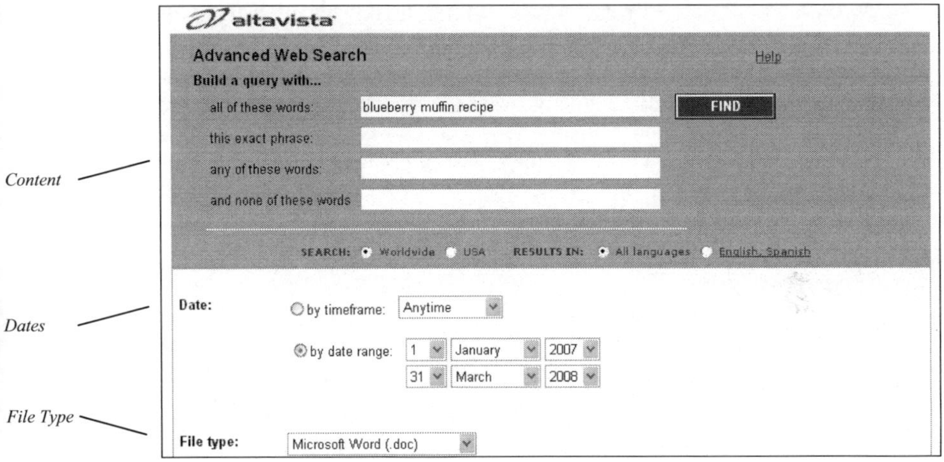

16. Click **Find**. All the matches are *Word* documents, created between the dates you specified.

There are many online reference books, encyclopaedias and dictionaries available such as ***www.webdictionary.co.uk****, which is free, and* ***www.Britannica.com****, which requires a subscription for full access.*

17. **Wikipedia** is a free encyclopaedia. Enter **www.wikipedia.org** in the **Address Bar** and on the home page, click the link for **English**. This is written by volunteers worldwide - beware - 100% accuracy cannot be guaranteed because of this, although topics are generally of a good quality.

18. In the **search** box, enter **blackbird** and click →. The information is retrieved and there are hyperlinks that lead to other, related topics.

19. Try a few more searches for topics that interest you.

Online dictionaries are also available, e.g. ***www.webdictionary.co.uk****.*

20. Click the **Home** button, , to return to your default **Home Page**.

Driving Lesson 25 - Subject Directories

Park and Read

There will be many occasions when a user wants to retrieve information from the web, but does not have a specific address. It is still possible to find relevant information by using a **subject directory**.

An alternative to a search engine, a **subject directory** classifies web sites by subject. Clicking on the relevant subject will take the user into progressively more detailed lists, from which a selection can be made. Advantages of using subject directories are that they generally contain good quality sites, consequently they contain fewer sites than search engines and therefore save time. Most of the search engines also contain these directories.

Manoeuvres

1. Enter the address **http://directory.google.com** in the **Address Bar**. Notice there is no **www** component to this address.

2. Scroll down below the **Search** box to find a list of subject categories.

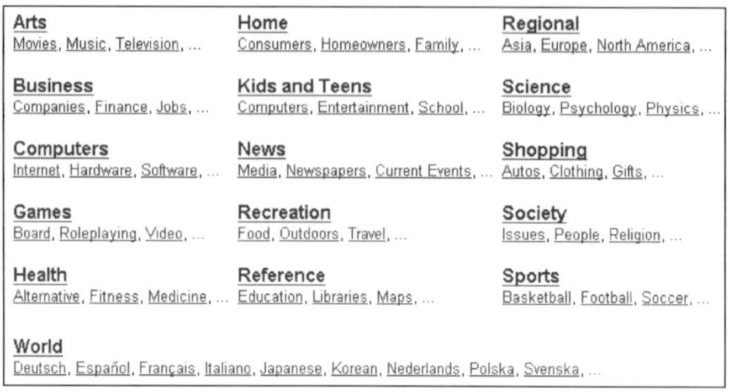

The screen may not match the one shown above

3. Under the **Arts** heading, click on the hyperlink **Movies**.

4. Select the **Actors and Actresses** category. An A-Z list will be displayed at the top of the page.

It is possible some of these links may have changed. If so, replace them with links of your choice.

5. Click on the letter **F**, then select the hyperlink **Fiennes, Ralph**.

6. Select any page from the list. Browse the page.

7. Click [Home button] to return to your default **Home Page**.

Driving Lesson 26 - The Search Bar

Park and Read

Explorer's **Search Bar** is a useful feature which speeds up the searching process. Once the bar is displayed, a search engine can be chosen from the options list.

Manoeuvres

1. Select **View | Explorer Bar | Search**. The **Search Bar** is displayed at the left of the screen.

*Alternatively the **Search Bar** can be displayed by clicking* 

.

2. Make sure **Find a Web page** is selected. Enter **holiday + greece** in the search box.
3. Click the **Search** button. By default, *Explorer* will use the **MSN Web Search** feature. After a few moments, a list of sites meeting the search criteria will be displayed in the **Search Bar**.
4. Visit a site from the list by clicking on its link in the list. It will be displayed on the right.
5. The site may not contain relevant information. Select a different site from the retrieval list, noting that it replaces the previous selection.

*As the **Search Bar** is always present, the user does not have to use the **Back** button to return to the list of search results. This means that, if a site selected from the retrieval list is unsuitable, a different site can quickly be selected from the **Search Bar**.*

6. Repeat step **5**.
7. Close the **Search Bar** by clicking on the **Close** button, ☒, next to its title.
8. Return to your default **Home Page**.

Driving Lesson 27 - Finding Text

Park and Read

Sometimes a web site may be found that seems to have the general content required, but it could have dozens (or even hundreds) of pages. It is not necessary for the user to view every page on the site to find out if it contains the information they want. *Internet Explorer* has a **Find** facility, which will search the document for specific text. **Find** is accessed by selecting the command **Edit | Find** to display the **Find** dialog box.

Manoeuvres

1. Go to the following address: **www.ciatraining.co.uk/downloads**.
2. Click the **About ECDL** hyperlink.
3. Select **Edit | Find (on this page)** or alternatively press <**Ctrl F**>. The **Find** dialog box appears. Clear any text in the **Find what** box from any previous search.

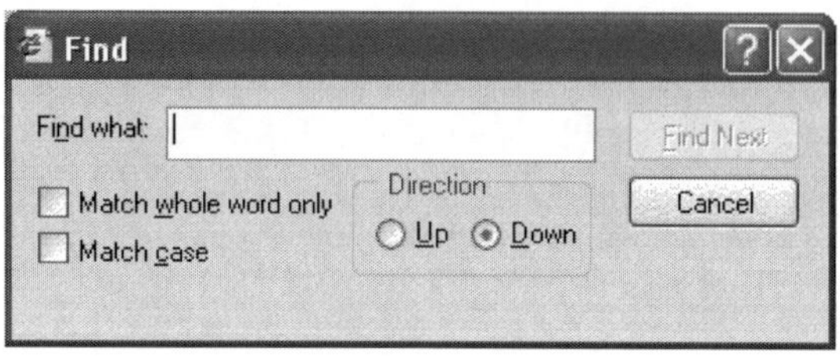

4. In the **Find what** box, enter **software**.
5. Select the option **Match whole word only**, then click **Find Next**. *Explorer* will highlight the first occurrence of the word **software** in the document.

*It may be necessary to move the **Find** dialog box to see the highlighted text - click and drag it by its blue **Title Bar**.*

6. Click **Find Next** again. Repeat this action until a message is displayed indicating that the search has been completed. Click **OK**.
7. Close the **Find** dialog box.
8. Go to your default **Home Page**.

Driving Lesson 28 - General Options

Park and Read

Explorer's **Internet Options** allow the user to change some of its elements to their individual preference, the default home page, for example, and the number of days pages are kept in the history, can be changed. Recently viewed pages are kept in a cache on the computer's hard drive, so that if they need to be viewed again they can be accessed quickly, without necessarily downloading them again. These **Temporary Internet files** can take up a lot of space on the hard drive, but can be deleted (if desired) from within **Internet Options**.

Many advertisers use windows that pop up in the middle of your screen. Some are helpful, but others can be annoying or can lead to downloading spyware or adware. *IE6* has an automatic pop-up blocker that gives some protection against this. **Cookies** (see Driving Lesson 3) can also be blocked or allowed.

Internet connection settings and the current program settings used by *Explorer* for e-mail and personal information can also be changed.

Manoeuvres

1. Select **Tools | Internet Options** to display the **Internet Options** dialog box. Select the **General** tab, if not already selected.

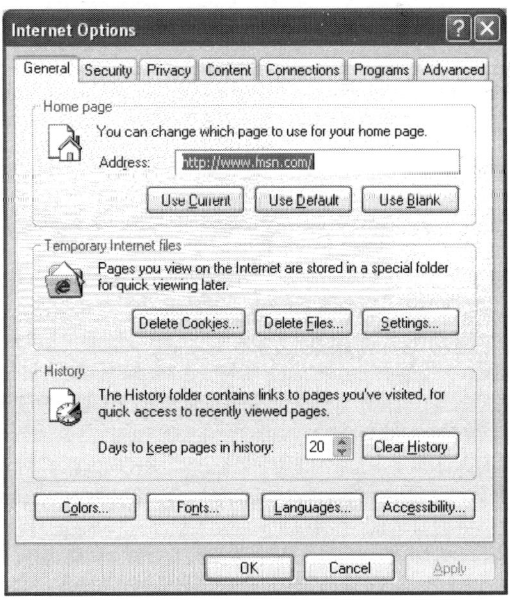

Driving Lesson 28 - Continued

2. In the **Home page** section, change the default address to **www.altavista.com**, then click **OK**.

3. Click . Note how the default **Home Page** is now **AltaVista**.

4. Display the **Internet Options** dialog box again. In the **Temporary Internet files** panel click **Delete Files**.

*To delete cookies, click the **Delete Cookies** button.*

5. Clicking on **OK** would remove all temporary files but as this would slow down subsequent actions, click **Cancel** to return to the dialog box.

6. Click on the **Colors** button and ensure that **Use Windows colors** is checked. Click **OK**.

7. Return the default home page to **Microsoft** by entering **www.msn.com** in the **Address** section of the **General** tab.

8. Look in the **History** panel. The **Days to keep pages in history** setting can be changed, if required. Entries in your **History** list of sites visited will be removed after the number of days set here. All entries on your **History** list can be deleted using the **Clear History** button.

9. Select the **Connections** tab and view the various connection options that are available. Do not change any of these settings.

10. Go back to the **General** tab and click **OK**.

11. To check pop-up blocker settings, select **Tools | Pop-up Blocker | Pop-up Blocker Settings**.

Driving Lesson 28 - Continued

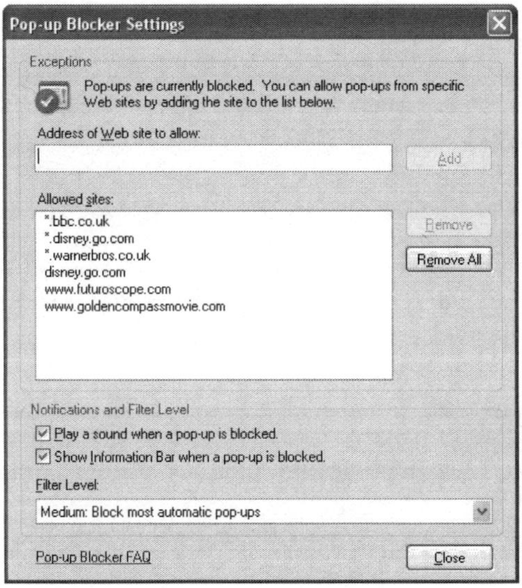

12. If you want to allow pop-ups from a particular web site, type the address into the box provided and click **Add**. To block pop-ups, select **High** from **Filter Level**.

*To temporarily allow pop-ups, click the **Information Bar**, when it tells you a pop-up has been blocked. Select **Temporarily Allow Pop-ups**.*

13. Click **Close** to remove the dialog box.

14. To see the settings for cookies, select **Tools | Internet Options** and the **Privacy** tab.

15. The **Privacy Settings** slider has 5 settings: **Block All Cookies**, **High**, **Medium High**, **Medium** (default), **Low** and **Accept All Cookies**. Choose the appropriate settings.

16. Click **Cancel** to close the dialog box without saving the changes in this instance.

17. Click **Home,**  and leave your default **Home Page** open.

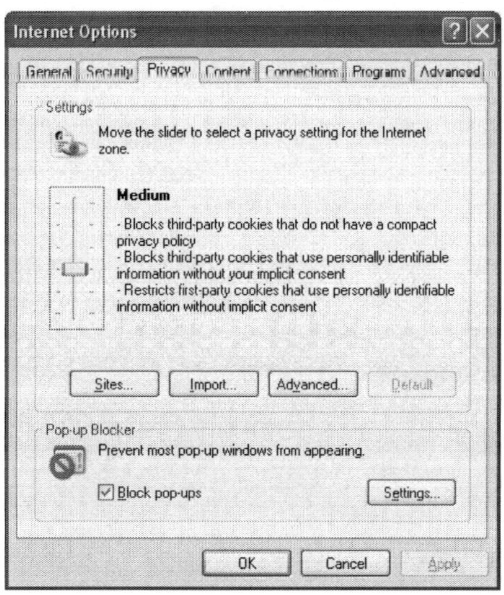

Driving Lesson 29 - Completing a Web Form

Park and Read

From time to time when you are using the Internet, especially if you are buying goods, it will be necessary to complete online forms. These forms can include **text boxes** (information is typed in), **drop down menus** (selection from a list), **check boxes** (items are selected or not) and **option buttons** (one selection only from a group).

There will also be a **Submit** button and a **Reset** or **Clear** button. The **Submit** button sends the form to its destination and the **Reset** button clears the form without sending it.

Manoeuvres

1. Go to **www.ciasupport.co.uk** using any method and click **here** to enter the site.
2. Click the **Online Forms** in the **Navigation** pane on the left.
3. Various online sample forms are available for completion from here. Read the text in the central frame then select **Feedback/Evaluation Form** on the left. A sample form is displayed in a new window.
4. This form includes various different methods of entering data; text boxes, drop down menus, check boxes and option selections. Complete the **Name** and **E-mail** text boxes.
5. Scroll down the form to the bottom then press the **Reset Form** button, [Reset Form]. All data is cleared from the form, ready to start again. This is used when mistakes have been made and it is easier to start again.
6. Re-enter the details, then complete the rest of the form. Entries with an * after them are essential and the form cannot be submitted without completing these fields.
7. When complete click the **Submit Form** button, [Submit Form].
8. Instead of transmitting the data this simulation displays a confirmation page. Close the **Form** window.
9. Return to your default **Home Page**.

Driving Lesson 30 - Revision

This covers the features introduced in this section. Try not to refer to the preceding Driving Lessons while completing it.

1. Change the default home page to **www.google.co.uk**.
2. Search for information on cheap flights to **Europe** using **Google**.
3. Display the **Search Bar**.
4. Search for information about **ECDL** (you will need to click 

if search details are already in the bar). Use the search criteria **"ECDL"**.
5. Were more or less than one million matches found?
6. Remove the **Search Bar** and go to **Alta Vista's** home page.
7. Enter the correct criteria to search for information about **hungarian recipes** <u>but not **goulash**</u>.
8. Were any matches found?
9. Use **russian** as the keyword and enter a search for **russian hamsters**.
10. View one of the matched pages and use the **Find** feature to see if you can find some information about their diet.
11. Return to **AltaVista** and search for web pages about your favourite film star or musician.
12. Change the default home page back to **msn.com**.

Check the answers at the back of the guide.

If you experienced any difficulty completing the Revision, refer back to the Driving Lessons in this section. Then redo the Revision.

Driving Lesson 31 - Revision

This covers the features introduced in this section. Try not to refer to the preceding Driving Lessons while completing it.

1. Go to **www.lycos.co.uk**.
2. Use search criteria to find **images** of the **Sahara Desert**.
3. Use any search engine to find out how to create a family tree.
4. Find out how to make a **tequila sunrise**.
5. See if you can find a web site dedicated to **Vietnamese pot bellied pigs**.
6. Bookmark the page.
7. Look for a web site specialising in holidays to **Iceland**.
8. Find out the cost of a return flight from **Heathrow** to **Paris**.
9. Go to your default **Home Page**.

If you experienced any difficulty completing the Revision, refer back to the Driving Lessons in this section. Then redo the Revision.

Once you are confident with the features, complete the Record of Achievement Matrix referring to the section at the end of the guide. Only when competent move on to the next Section.

Section 4
Saving and Printing

By the end of this Section you should be able to:

Save a Web Page

Duplicate Web Page Items

Modify Page Setup

Preview and Print a Page

Print a Search Result

Download Files

To gain an understanding of the above features, work through the **Driving Lessons** in this **Section**.

For each **Driving Lesson**, read the **Park and Read** instructions, without touching the keyboard, then work through the numbered steps of the **Manoeuvres** on the computer. Complete the **Revision Exercise(s)** at the end of the section to test your knowledge.

Driving Lesson 32 - Saving a Web Page

Park and Read

Web pages can be saved directly from the Internet in the same way as other files or folders, either on the hard drive or floppy drive of the computer.

Manoeuvres

1. Use the **Address Bar** list to go to **www.ciatraining.co.uk/downloads**.
2. Click on the **Images** hyperlink. To save this web page, select **File | Save as** from the menu. The **Save Web Page** dialog box will appear.
3. In the **Save in** box, specify the location where the file is to be saved, in this case **My Documents**.

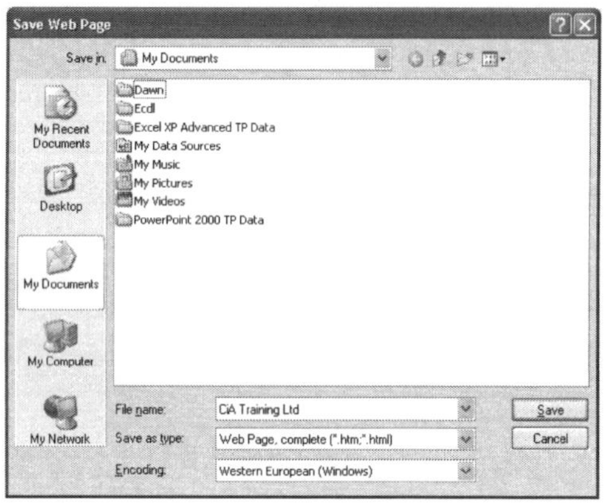

4. Make sure **Save as type** shows **Web Page, complete**.
5. Change the **File name** to **Images** by overtyping the existing name and click **Save**.
6. Click on the **Downloads** link in the navigation frame.
7. Right click on the hyperlink text **Profile.txt** and select **Save Target As** from the shortcut menu.
8. Select **My Documents** as the saving location. From **Save as type** select **Text Document** and click **Save**.
9. Click **Close** if a **Download Complete** dialog box appears. Minimise *Explorer* and select **My Documents** from the **Desktop** or the **Start** menu.
10. The **Images** file should be there, as an HTML file,  and the **Profile** text file will be there too, .
11. Double click the **Images** file name and it will be displayed in its own *Explorer* window without the need for an Internet connection, i.e. offline.
12. Close the new *Explorer* window and **My Documents**.
13. Maximise the original *Explorer* window and leave the page open for the next Driving Lesson.

Driving Lesson 33 - Copying Web Page Items

Park and Read

It is possible to copy text and images from a web page and then to paste them into a document.

Manoeuvres

1. Go to the **CiA Training** page, **www.ciatraining.co.uk/downloads**.
2. Click the **Images** hyperlink at the left of the page. To copy the big banana, right click on it and select **Copy** from the shortcut menu.
3. Start *Word* (**Start | All Programs | Microsoft Word**).
4. Click **Paste**, or press <**Ctrl V**>, to place the copied image in the document.

5. Press <**Enter**> to start a new line and use the **Taskbar** to return to the **CiA** site.
6. Click and drag to highlight the address, the full **URL** in the **Address Bar**.
7. Right click and select **Copy** from the shortcut menu or press <**Ctrl C**>.
8. Switch back to *Word*. Type in **Why not try visiting** and then click **Paste** to complete the sentence.
9. The address of the **CiA** web page is pasted into the document. Press <**Backspace**> to remove the final backslash character from the address then press <**Spacebar**>. Notice how the address becomes blue, indicating that it is now a hyperlink.
10. Click the hyperlink to go to the web page (in *Word* it may also be necessary to hold down the **Ctrl** key). There may be a message recommending saving the *Word* document, if so click **No**. Notice on the **Taskbar** that another *IE* window has been opened to display the page.
11. Close this new *IE* window.
12. Click and drag to select the text above the pictures on the **Images** page.
13. Copy the text and switch back to *Word*.
14. Press <**Enter**> and paste in the copied text.
15. Save the document in **My Documents** as **Copied** and close *Word*.

Driving Lesson 34 - Page Setup

Park and Read

If necessary, the **Page Setup** (margins, etc.) of a web page can be changed before printing. You may occasionally want to change the size of paper used, e.g. to **A5**. This will mean the settings must also be adjusted to print the information in the correct position on the paper.

Manoeuvres

1. Make sure you are viewing the **www.ciatraining.co.uk/downloads** page and click the **Home Page** link to go to the home page of the **CIA** web site.

2. Select **File | Page Setup** to display the following dialog box:

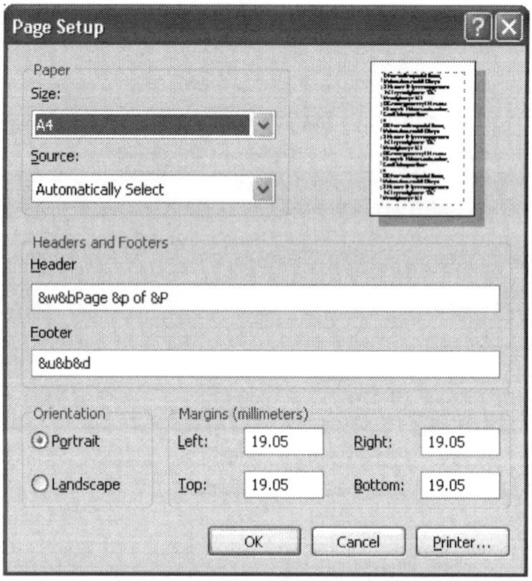

3. Look at the available settings. Change the **Orientation** of the printed page by selecting the **Landscape** option from the bottom of the dialog box.

4. Change all margins: **Left**, **Right**, **Top** and **Bottom** to **25mm** by deleting the number in the boxes and entering the new measurement.

5. To change the size of paper used click the drop down arrow at the right of the **Size** box. Select **A5 (148 x 210mm)**. This option depends on the default printer, if unavailable select any other size.

*Printer settings can be changed by clicking the **Printer** button.*

6. Click **OK** to apply the new settings and move on to the next Driving Lesson.

Driving Lesson 35 - Printing a Web Page

Park and Read

IE6 can print pages, or parts of pages, directly from the Internet. The user can decide exactly which parts of the web page to print. If the page is **framed**, individual frames or selected frames can be printed, or the page can be printed as it appears on the screen. It is also possible to print all linked documents, or a table of links. A page can be previewed before printing.

Manoeuvres

1. With the **CiA Training** home page on screen, select **File | Print Preview**. A preview of how the page will appear is displayed. Click **Close** to remove the preview.

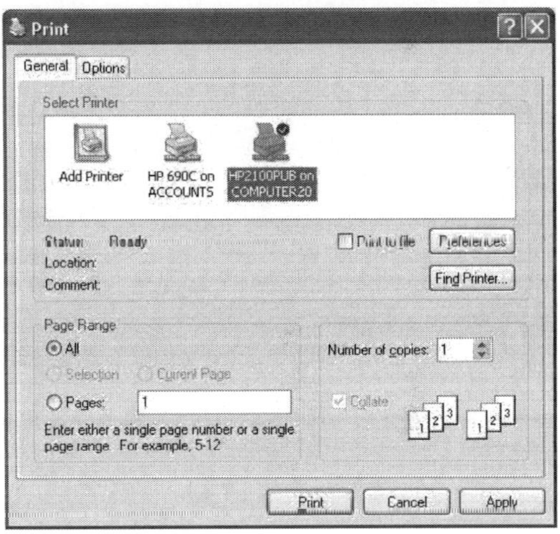

2. Select **File | Print** or press <**Ctrl P**> to display the **Print** dialog box.

3. Select the appropriate printer and in the **Print range** section, select to print page **1** only, and make sure that the **Number of copies** is set to **1**.

*The **Selection** option is ghosted unless a selection from the page has already been made.*

4. Under the **Options** tab, make sure that the check boxes **Print all linked documents** and **Print table of links** are either unchecked (not ticked) or ghosted. Opt to print the frames **As laid out on screen** from the **Print frames** section. Click **Print**.

*The **Print** button, , can be used to print a single copy of the page to the default printer without displaying the **Print** dialog box.*

5. Click the **About ECDL** link. When the page is displayed, click and drag across the first paragraph of text to highlight it in blue.

6. To print only the selected text, select **File | Print**. From **Page Range** choose **Selection** and click **Print**.

7. Click the **Home** button, .

Driving Lesson 36 - Printing a Search Result

Park and Read

If a list of search results has been retrieved and the user does not wish to spend online time ploughing through them, the results can be printed. This means that any appropriate sites can be marked, then browsed at a later time.

Manoeuvres

1. Use any search engine and enter the following search: **"Garden gnomes"**.
2. When a list of matching sites is retrieved, check the number of pages found (you may not want to print hundreds!). An example is shown below.

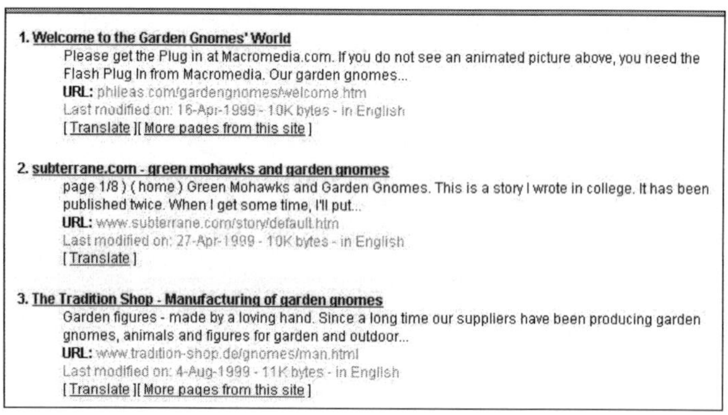

3. Select **File | Page Setup** and change the **Orientation** back to **Portrait**.
4. Select **File | Print** or press <**Ctrl P**>.
5. Select to print the range of pages **1** to **3**, by selecting the **Pages** option and typing **1-3** in the box.
6. Click **Print**.
7. Make sure your default **Home Page** is displayed.

Driving Lesson 37 - Downloading Files

Park and Read

Many types of files, including sound and video files can be downloaded from the Internet and viewed or played. Downloaded files can also be permanently saved to either the hard or floppy disk of the computer in a variety of ways.

Manoeuvres

1. Go to **www.ciatraining.co.uk/downloads**.
2. Click the **Downloads** hyperlink at the left of the page to display the following page.

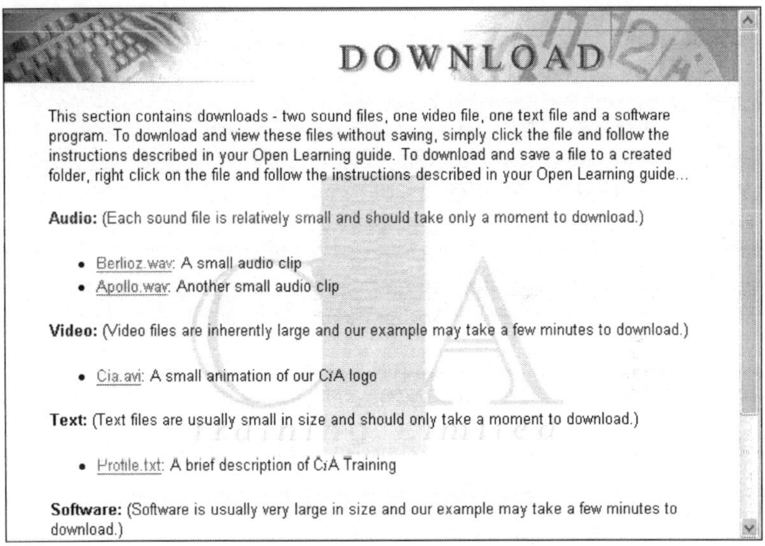

3. Click on the hyperlink **Berlioz.wav**. By default the **Media Bar** will open on the left of the *Explorer* window and the file will start to download. There may be a dialog box asking if you want to play the item within Internet Explorer, if so click **Yes**.

*If a different application such as **Realplayer** has been set up to be the default media player, then that application will be started in a separate window, ready to play the downloaded file. The controls may vary between different media players but will be functionally similar.*

Driving Lesson 37 - Continued

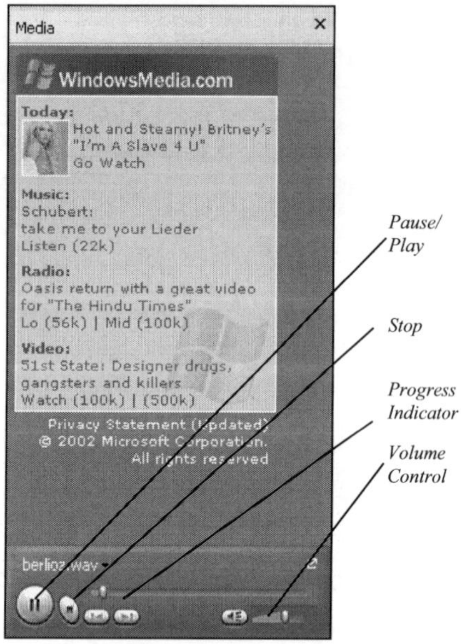

4. As the sound is downloading, it will play (possibly with some interference). When the download is complete, the **Pause** button becomes the **Play** button. Press this to hear the music again.

5. Close the **Media Bar** and click the **Images** hyperlink from the **ciatraining** page.

6. Right click on the image of the big banana and select **Save Picture As** from the shortcut menu.

7. In the **Save Picture** dialog box make sure **Save in** is set to **My Pictures**, **File name** as **banana** and **Save as type** is set to **GIF[*.gif]**. Click **Save**.

8. Minimise *IE* and from the desktop open **My Documents** then **My Pictures**. A copy of the image has been downloaded into the **My Pictures** folder on the hard disk and will remain there until deleted, even after the Internet connection has been closed.

9. Right click on the banana image in **My Pictures** and select **Delete**. Select **Yes** from the confirmation box to remove the image. Close the **My Pictures** window and maximize the *IE* window.

The sound file could have been permanently downloaded in a similar manner by right clicking on the ***Berlioz.wav*** *hyperlink and selecting* ***Save Target As*** *from the shortcut menu.*

10. Click the **Downloads** link again. To download some software click the **Notes.exe** link at the bottom of the page.

11. At the **File Download** prompt, click **Save**. Choose **My Documents** as the saving location and click **Close** when the **Download Complete** message appears.

12. View **My Documents** to see the icon,  . Double click it to start the demonstration program.

13. Close the **notes** program and delete the icon from **My Documents**.

14. Close **My Documents**.

Driving Lesson 38 - Revision

This covers the features introduced in this section. Try not to refer to the preceding Driving Lessons while completing it.

1. Go to the **NASA** home page (**www.nasa.gov**).
2. Use hyperlinks to find a page that interests you.
3. Save the web page as a file.
4. Use **AltaVista** to search for web pages about homeopathy.
5. Print the first two pages only of the search result.
6. Go to www.ciatraining.co.uk.
7. Change the page orientation to **Landscape**.
8. Print one copy of page **1**.

In the ***Print*** *dialog box, pages refer to printed pages, not web pages. For example one web page may take up 3 printed pages. Printing page 1 produces one printed page, which may not be the whole web page.*

9. Go to **www.ciatraining.co.uk/downloads** (adding **/downloads** to the existing address will work) and click the **Downloads** link.
10. Download the **Cia.avi** video clip.
11. Save the **Apollo.wav** sound file in **My Documents**.
12. View the web page saved from the **NASA** site in step 3.
13. Close any open programs and disconnect from the Internet.

If you experienced any difficulty completing the Revision, refer back to the Driving Lessons in this section. Then redo the Revision.

Driving Lesson 39 - Revision

This covers the features introduced in this section. Try not to refer to the preceding Driving Lessons while completing it.

1. Go to **www.nasa.gov**
2. Right click on any image.
3. Save the image in **My Pictures** as **nasapic**.
4. Choose a link to another page and save the resulting web page in **My Documents** as **nasapage**.
5. Return to your **Home** page.
6. Open **My Pictures** and display the image **nasapic**.
7. Close the image and delete it from **My Pictures**.
8. Open **My Documents** and display the page **nasapage**.
9. Close the page and delete it from **My Documents**.
10. Close any open windows.
11. Close *IE6*, disconnecting if you have a dial up connection.

If you experienced any difficulty completing the Revision, refer back to the Driving Lessons in this section. Then redo the Revision.

Once you are confident with the features, complete the Record of Achievement Matrix referring to the section at the end of the guide. Only when competent move on to the next Section.

Answers

Driving Lesson 11

Step 1 **www** stands for **world wide web**.

Step 2 The programming language used on the Internet is **HTML**.

Step 3 Traditionally, a connection (usually a telephone line), a modem and ISP (Internet Service Provider), although Broadband connections now allow more direct access using devices other than modems.

Step 5 The **Search**, **Favorites** and **History** buttons can be used to change the view of the screen.

Step 6 Framed web pages are used to improve navigation around a web site.

Driving Lesson 12

Step 2 The Internet is a world wide network connection of computers.

Step 3 The world wide web refers to the information that exists on the Internet.

Step 4 **Cookies** are small text files that are stored on your computer when you visit a web site.

Step 5 **Encrypted** means scrambled. Can only be deciphered with a key.

Step 6 A **firewall** is a program that protects a computer from unauthorised access via the Internet.

Step 7 Secure servers are identified by a small padlock in the **Status Bar**.

Driving Lesson 30

Step 5 More than one million.

Step 8 Yes, many thousand.

Glossary

Address Bar	Shows the address of the page currently displayed in the Browser and allows entry of a new address to be visited.
Browser	The application that controls your interface with the World Wide Web.
Dial-up Connection	A method of connecting to the Internet that requires a modem on the computer dialling the number of a server.
Download	Transfers an object from an web site to the users computer.
Favorites	A list of selected web pages that can be visited with a single mouse click.
Folder	A method of grouping together files (and other folders).
Frames	Separate areas of a single web page that each act like individual pages.
History	A list of web pages visited recently.
Home Page (1)	The main page in a site, with links to all other pages.
Home Page (2)	Your Home Page is the page displayed when the Browser starts and when you press the Home button.
Hyperlink	Area of a page which can be clicked to move to a different location, usually a different web page.
Link	Abbreviation for **Hyperlink**.
Media Player	An application which plays sound or video files.
Multimedia	An application or function that involves many techniques such as text, sound and video.
Navigation	Moving around between web sites or the pages within a site.
Offline	Without having a current connection to the Internet.
Online	Having a current connection to the Internet.
Page Range	The specific print pages to be included when printing out a large web page.
Recycle Bin	An area of storage where deleted files are held temporarily before being deleted completely.
Refresh	Redisplays the most recent version of the current page.
Search Engine	A web site that allows all other sites to be searched for specified topics.
Subfolder	A folder that is contained within another folder.

Index

Record of Achievement Matrix

This Matrix is to be used to measure your progress while working through the guide. This is a learning reinforcement process, you judge when you are competent.

Tick boxes are provided for each feature. 1 is for no knowledge, 2 some knowledge and 3 is for competent. A section is only complete when column 3 is completed for all parts of the section.

For details on sitting ECDL Examinations in your country please contact the local ECDL Licensee or visit the European Computer Driving Licence Foundation Limited web site at http://www.ecdl.com.

Tick the Relevant Boxes **1**: No Knowledge **2**: Some Knowledge **3**: Competent

Section	No	Driving Lesson	1	2	3
1 Getting Started	1	Internet Theory			
	2	Internet Explorer			
	3	Security on the Internet			
	4	Connecting to the Internet			
	5	Dial-up Connection			
	6	Browser Help			
	7	Internet Explorer Screen			
	8	Views			
	9	Framed Web Pages			
	10	Closing the Browser			
2 Navigation	13	Using Hyperlinks			
	14	Back and Forward Buttons			
	15	Using Web Addresses			
	16	Bookmarks			
	17	Organising Bookmarks			
	18	The Links Bar			
	19	Browsing History			
	20	Stop and Refresh Downloads			
3 Browsing the Web	23	Search Engines			
	24	Search Criteria			
	25	Subject Directories			
	26	The Search Bar			
	27	Finding Text			
	28	General Options			
	29	Completing a Web Form			
4 Saving and Printing	32	Saving a Web Page			
	33	Copying Web Page Items			
	34	Page Setup			
	35	Printing a Web Page			
	36	Printing a Search Result			
	37	Downloading Files			

Other Products from CiA Training Ltd

CiA Training Ltd is a leading publishing company, which has consistently delivered the highest quality products since 1985. A wide range of flexible and easy to use self teach resources has been developed by CiA's experienced publishing team to aid the learning process. These include the following ECDL Foundation approved products at the time of publication of this product:

- **ECDL/ICDL Syllabus 5.0**
- **ECDL/ICDL Advanced Syllabus 2.0**
- **ECDL/ICDL Revision Series**
- **ECDL/ICDL Advanced Syllabus 2.0 Revision Series**
- **e-Citizen**

Previous syllabus versions also available - contact us for further details.

We hope you have enjoyed using our materials and would love to hear your opinions about them. If you'd like to give us some feedback, please go to:

www.ciatraining.co.uk/feedback.php

and let us know what you think.

New products are constantly being developed. For up to the minute information on our products, to view our full range, to find out more, or to be added to our mailing list, visit:

www.ciatraining.co.uk

Notes

Notes